PreK-K

Scott Foresman

Patterns

Simple Patterns to Color and Cut Out

PEARSON

Scott Foresman

Editorial Offices: Glenview, Illinois • Parsippany, New Jersey • New York, New York
Sales Offices: Needham, Massachusetts • Duluth, Georgia • Glenview, Illinois
Coppell, Texas • Sacramento, California • Mesa, Arizona

Contents

4

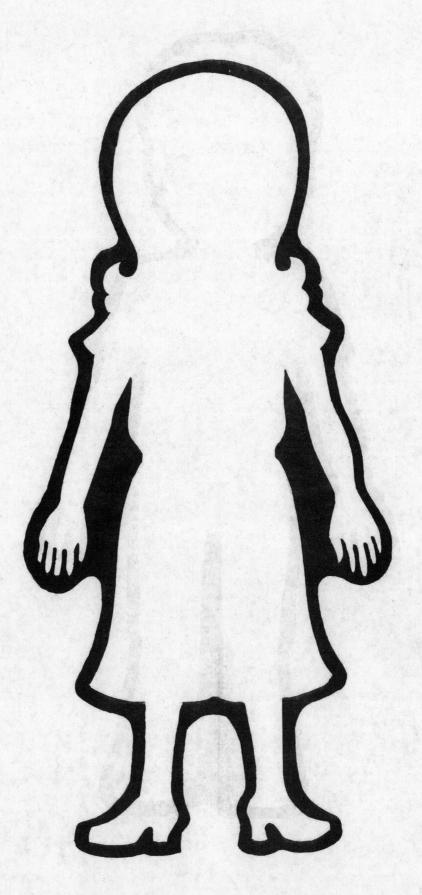

8

16

25

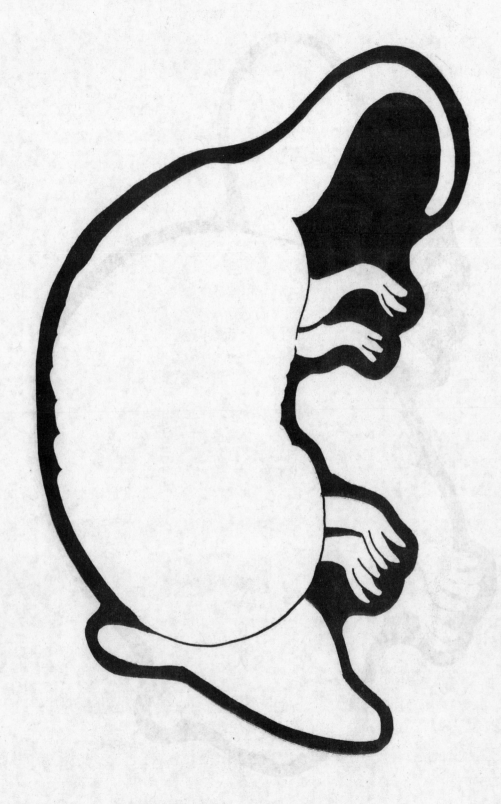

28

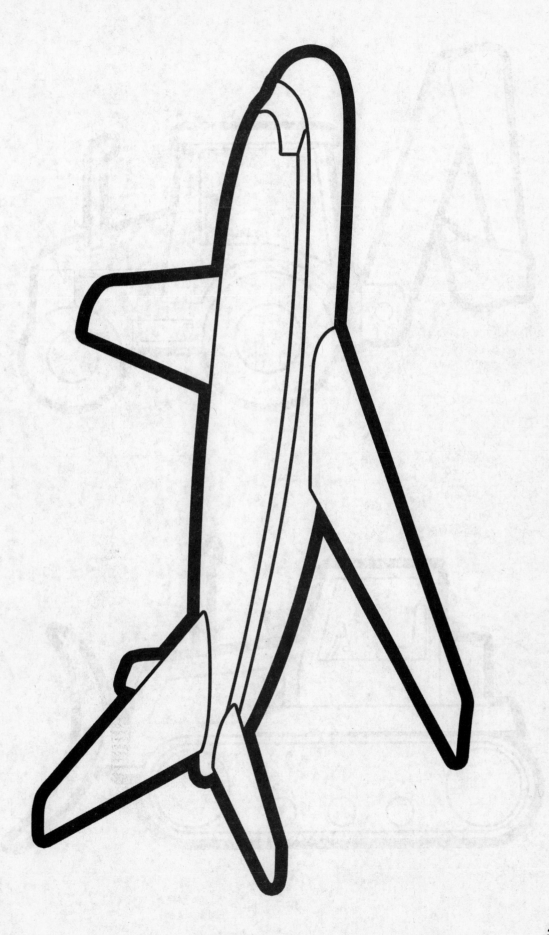

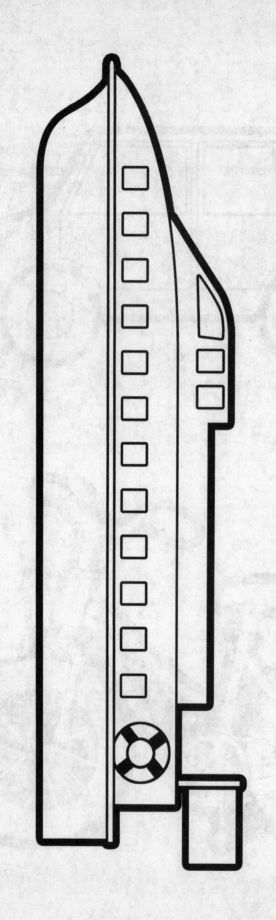

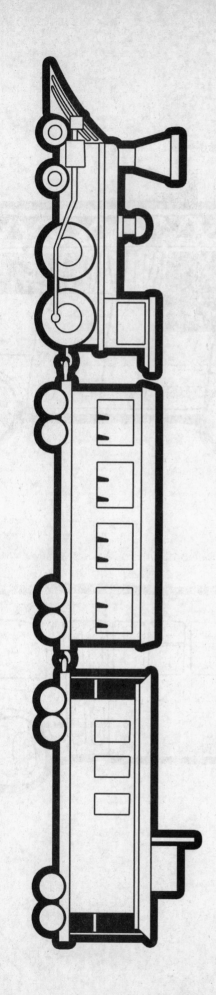

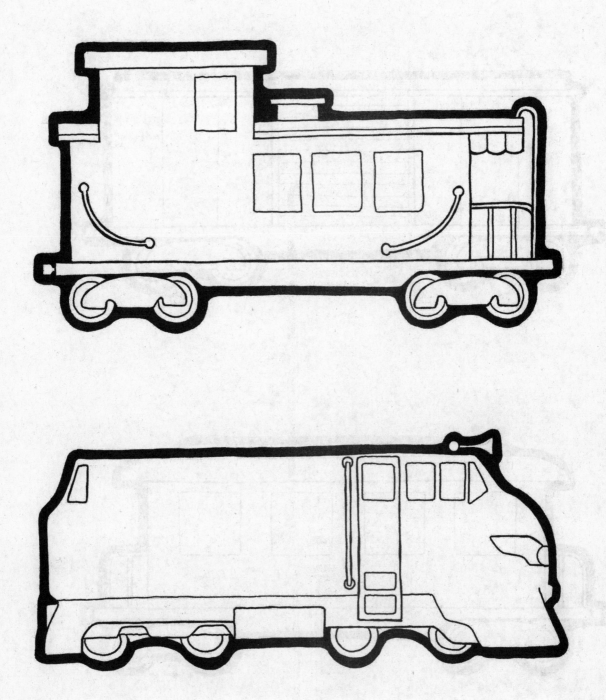

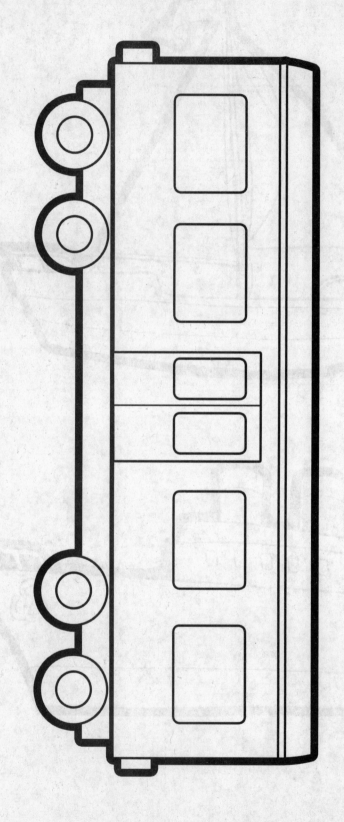

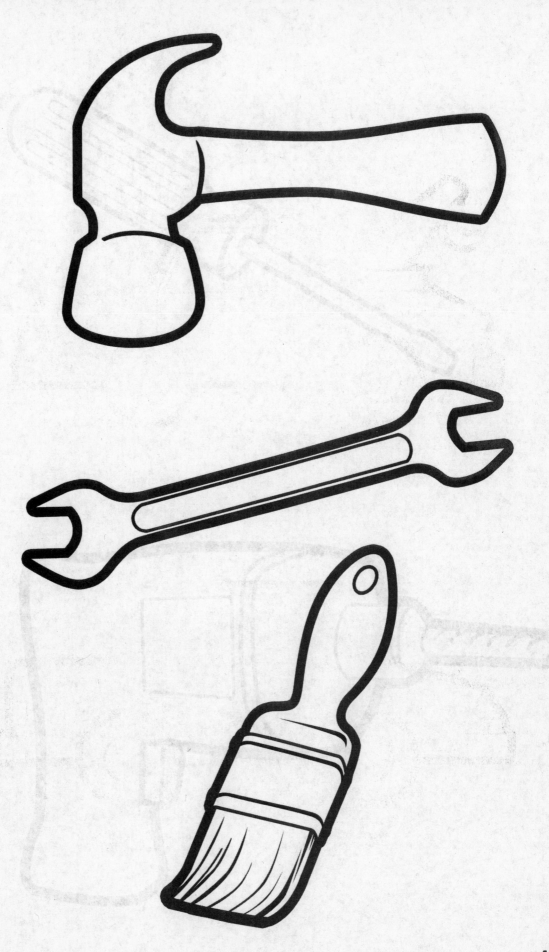

45

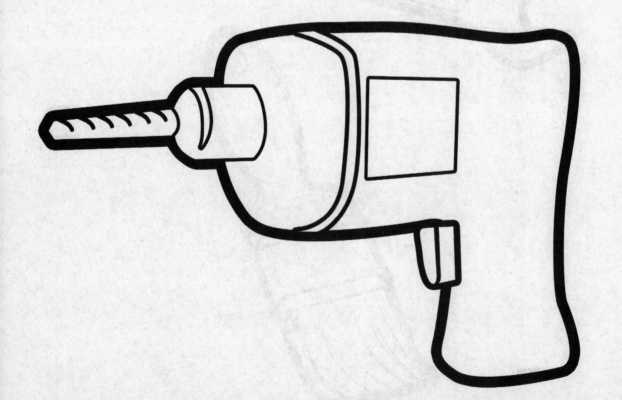

58

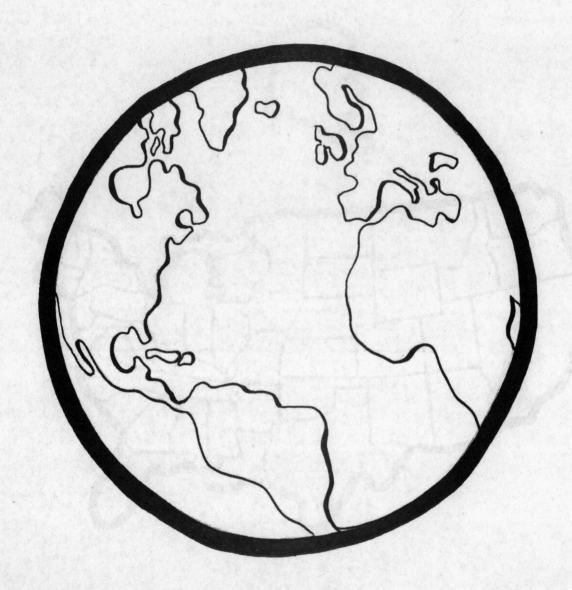